PIANO / VOCAL / GUITAR

TOP COUNTRY HITS 2009-2010

ISBN 978-1-4234-7615-3

7777 W. Bluemound Rd. P.O. Box 13819 Milwaukee, WI 53213

Visit Hal Leonard Online at
www.halleonard.com

AMERICAN RIDE

Words and Music by JOE WEST
and DAVE PAHANISH

A
get bust - ed sing - in' Christ - mas car - ols.
Liv - in' in a cruel world, pays to be a mean girl.
N.C.
E
D
That's us, that's right,
A
E
got - ta love this A - mer - i - can ride. Both ends of the
D
A
E
o - zone burn - in', fun - ny how the world keeps turn - in'.

D
A
(1.,2.) Look, ma, no hands,
(D.S.) Hot dog, hot damn,
I love
this A - mer - i - can
E
D
ride.
To Coda
A
E
E5
Got - ta love this A - mer - i - can ride.
D5
5fr
A
1
E5

2
E5
B
Poor lit - tle in - fa - "Miss" A - mer - i - ca's down; she
A
E
B
gained five pounds and lost her crown. Quick fix, plas - tic
A
sur - gi - cal an - ti - dote; got her - self a rec - ord deal,
N.C.
E5
can't e - ven sing a note. Plas - ma get - tin' big - ger,

D5
5fr
A5
5fr
Je - sus get - tin' small - er, spill a cup o' cof - fee,
E5
make a mil - lion dol - lars. Cus - toms caught a thug with an
D5
5fr
A
aer - o - sol can. If the shoe don't fit, the fit's gon - na hit the shan.
D.S. al Coda
N.C.

CODA
E
E5
D5
5fr
mer - i - can ride.
A
E5
Na na na
D5
5fr
A
E5
na na na na, na na na na na na na.
D5
5fr
A
E5
Na na na na na na na, na na na na na.

AMERICAN SATURDAY NIGHT

Words and Music by BRAD PAISLEY,
KELLEY LOVELACE and ASHLEY GORLEY

A
E
A
"Back in the U. S. S. R."
Yeah, she's go -
E
A
E
- in' 'round the world to - night, but she ain't leav - in' here.
A
E
A
She's just goin' to meet her boy - friend down at the street fair.
E
A
E
And it's a French kiss,

A
E
A
I - tal - ian ice,
Span - ish moss in the moon - light,
E
B
A
E
just an - oth - er A - mer - i - can Sat - ur - day night.
A
E
A
There's a
E
A
E
big to - ga par - ty to - night down at Del - ta Chi.

A
E
A
They got Ca - na - di - an ba - con on their piz - za pie.
E
A
E
They got a cool - er full of cold Co - ro -
A
E
A
- nas and Am - stel Light.
It's like
B
A
we're all liv - in' in a big ol' cup, just fire up the blend - er and

B
E
A
mix it all up. It's a French kiss, I - tal - ian ice,
E
A
E
mar - ga - ri - tas in the moon - light,
just an - oth - er A - mer -
B
A
E
i - can Sat - ur - day night.
You know ev -
C♯m
4fr
B
A
E
- 'ry - where has some - thin' they're known for,

C♯m
4fr
B
E
al-though u - sual - ly it wash - es up on our
A
shores.
My great - great - great - grand - dad -
Lit - tle It - a - ly and Chi -
To Coda
E
B
E
- dy stepped off of that ship.
na - town, sit - tin' there side by side.
I bet he
A
E
B
B/A
nev - er ev - er dreamed we'd have all this.

G♯m
B/F♯
E
A
E
A
E
B
A
E
D.S. al Coda
You know ev -
CODA
E
A
Live from New
B
N.C.
E
A
York, It's a French kiss, I - tal - ian ice,
(it's Sat - ur - day night!)

E
A
E
Span - ish moss in the moon - light.
Just an - oth - er A - mer -
B
A
E
A
i - can,
just an - oth - er A - mer - i - can,
it's
E
B
A
E
E
just an - oth - er A - mer - i - can Sat - ur - day night.
A
E
A
Repeat and Fade
Optional Ending
E

BIG GREEN TRACTOR

Words and Music by JIM COLLINS
and DAVID LEE MURPHY

C♯m
4fr
A
dogs were all bark - in' and a wag - gin' a - round, and I just laughed and said, "You
B
E
all get in." She had on a new dress and she curled her hair. She was
"We can fire it up and I can show you a - round.
B/D♯
4fr
look - in' too good not to go some - where. Said,
Sit up on the hill and watch the sun go down. When the
C♯m
4fr
"What you wan - na do, ba - by? I don't care. We can
fire - flies are danc - in' and the moon comes out, we can

A
B
go to the show, we can stay out here, and I can
turn on the lights and head back to the house, or we can
E
B
take you for a
take an - oth - er
ride on my big green trac - tor. We can go slow or
F♯m7
make it go fast - er, down through the woods and out to the pas - ture.
A
B
E
Long as I'm with you, it real - ly don't mat - ter. Climb up in my lap
(D.S.) climb up in my lap
and

B
drive if you want to. Girl, you know you got me to hold__ on to.
F♯m7
E/G♯
To Coda
1
A
We can go to town, but ba - by, if you'd rath - er, I'll take you for a ride on my
E
big green trac - tor."
B
2
A
Said, take you for a ride on my

B
C♯m
4fr
big green trac - tor.
And just let me dust
A
B
C♯m
4fr
off the seat.
Mm,
B
uh, put your pret - ty lit - tle arms a - round me.
E
B/D♯
4fr
3

C♯m
4fr
3
A
B
D.S. al Coda
And you can
CODA
A
take you for a ride on my
big green trac - tor.
B
Whoa, yeah, yeah.
E
B

F♯m
We can go to town
A
B
E
or we can go an - oth - er round
B
on my big green
F♯m7
E/G♯
A
trac - tor."

BONFIRE

Words and Music by KEVIN DENNEY, CRAIG MORGAN,
TOM BOTKIN and MIKE ROGERS

A
D/A
A7
- cov - ered trucks and S - U - V's crank - in' up Hank and A -
popped a top and hol - lered real loud, "Don't wor - ry, y'all. I came
- C - D - C.
to hang out."
D7
At the bon - fire out
C
G7
C
G7
in the sticks, coun - try back - woods, home - grown hicks.
D7
C
G7
Bon - fire, dance a lit - tle jig, hold up your cup and take

C
G7
N.C.
A
an - oth - er swig.
Won't
sleep till dawn, gon - na
D/A
G
par - ty right down to the wire
at the
1
D7
bon - fire.
Ev - 'ry -
2
D7
C
bon - fire.

G7
D7

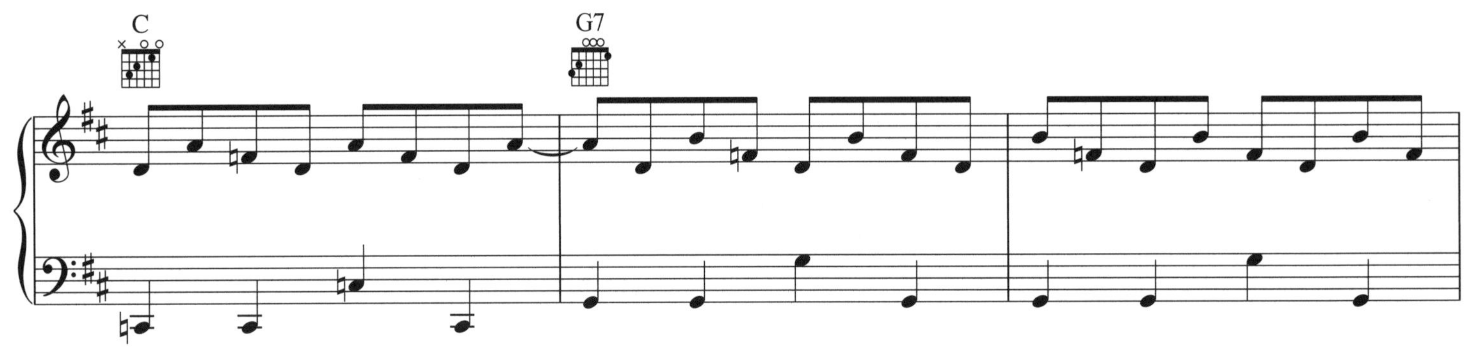
C
G7

F
N.C.
You don't have to be from a - round here to know right where

to go.
F
N.C.
All you got - ta do is load up and

G7
head towards the glow.
D7
C
At the bon - fire out in the sticks,
G7
C
G7
D7
coun - try back - woods, home - grown hicks. Bon - fire, dance
C
1
G7
a lit - tle jig, hold up your cup and take an - oth - er swig. At the

2
G7
C
G7
N.C.
hold up your cup and take an - oth - er swig.
A
D/A
Won't sleep till dawn, gon - na par - ty right down to the
G
G7
wire
D7
C
at the bon - fire.

G7 C G7 D7

We're all hang - in' at the bon - fire.

C G7 C G7

N.C.

COWBOY CASANOVA

Words and Music by MIKE ELIZONDO,
BRETT JAMES and CARRIE UNDERWOOD

Dm
N.C.
run and you try and you're try - in' to hide and you're won - der - ing why you can't get free.
He's like a curse, he's like a drug.
You get ad - dict - ed to his love.
You
wan - na get out, but he's hold - in' you down 'cause you can't live with - out one more touch.

A
C
Dm
C/E
He's a, a good - time cow -
F
B♭
A
- boy Ca - sa - no - va lean - ing up a - gainst the rec - ord ma - chine.
Dm
C/E
F
B♭
He looks like a cool drink of wa - ter, but he's can - dy - coat - ed mis - er - y.
A
Dm
C/E
F
He's a dev - il in dis - guise, a snake with blue eyes and he

Gm7
A
B♭
on - ly comes out at night.
Gives you feel - ings that you don't wan - na fight.
C
N.C.
To Coda
You bet - ter run for your life.
Oh,
oh.
I see that look on your face.
You ain't hear - ing what I

say.
So, I'll say it a-gain 'cause I been where you been and I
know how it ends, you can't get a-way.
F
E♭
3fr
Don't e-ven look in his eyes.
N.C.
He'll tell you noth-ing but lies.
And you wan-na be-lieve, but you won't be de-ceived if you

A
C
D.S. al Coda
listen to me and take my advice.
He's a,
CODA
Dm
D5
5fr
Run, run a - way,
D7(no3)
G/D
Gm/D
don't let him mess with your mind.
He'll tell you an - y - thing you wan - na hear.

D5
5fr
D7(no3)
G/D
He'll break your heart, it's just a mat - ter of time. But just
Gm/D
N.C.
F
re - mem - ber he's a, a good - time cow - boy Ca - sa - no - va lean - ing
B♭
A
Dm
C/E
up a - gainst the rec - ord ma - chine. He looks like a cool
F
B♭
A
drink of wa - ter, but he's can - dy - coat - ed mis - er - y. He's a

Dm
C/E
F
Gm7
dev - il in dis - guise, a snake with blue eyes and he on - ly comes out at night.
A
B♭
C
N.C.
Gives you feel - ings that you don't wan - na fight. You bet - ter run for your life.
Oh, you bet - ter run for your life.
Oh, you bet - ter run for your
life.

DO I

Words and Music by LUKE BRYAN,
DAVE HAYWOOD and CHARLES KELLEY

F♯m7
E
or act like I don't e - ven know you.
Seems like you could care less ei - ther way.
D
A/C♯
Bm7
A
What hap - pened to that girl
E/G♯
Bm7
A
I used to know?
I just want us back to the
E/G♯
E
E/G♯
A
way we were be - fore.
Do I turn you on at all when I kiss you, ba - by? Does the

F♯m7
D
sight of me want- in' you drive you cra - zy? Do I have your love? Am I still e - nough? Tell me
Bm7
E
A
don't I or tell me do I, ba - by, give you ev -'ry - thing that you ev - er want - ed? Would you
F♯m7
D
A/C♯
To Coda
rath - er just turn a - way and leave me lone - ly? Do I just need to give up and get on with my
Bm7
E
A
life? Ba - by, do I?

F♯m7(add4)
Esus
E
A
F♯m7
Re-mem-ber when we did-n't have noth - in'
but a per-fect, sim-ple kind of lov - in'?
E
D
A/C♯
Ba - by, those sure were the days.
Bm7
A
E/G♯
E
There was a time our love ran wild and free.

D.S. al Coda
Bm7
A
E/G♯
E
E/G♯
But now I'm sec - ond guess - in' ev - 'ry - thing I see. Do I
CODA
Bm7
E
F♯m7
life? Ba - by, do I still give
Esus
E
D
you what you need, still take your breath a - way, and light up a spark
Bm7
E
A
way down deep? Ba - by, do I?
3

F#m7
D
Bm7
E
A
Whoa, do I turn you on at all when I kiss you, ba - by? Does the
sight of me want-in' you drive you cra - zy? Do I have your love? Am I still e-nough? Tell me
N.C.
don't I or tell me do I, ba - by, give you ev-'ry-thing that you ev - er want - ed? Would you

F♯m7
D
A/C♯
rath-er just turn a-way and leave me lone - ly? Do I just need to give up and get on with my
Bm7
A/C♯
D
A/C♯
life? Tell me, ba - by, do I get one more try?
Bm7
Esus
E
A
Do I?
F♯m7(add4)
Esus
D
Asus2
Ba - by, do I?
rit.

FIFTEEN

Words and Music by
TAYLOR SWIFT

Csus2
3fr
Em7
seen in a while, try and stay out of ev - 'ry - bod - y's way.
Csus2
3fr
G
It's your fresh - man year and you're
Csus2
3fr
Em7
gon - na be here for the next four years in this
Csus2
3fr
G
town. Hop - in' one of those sen - ior boys will

Csus2
3fr
Em7
wink at you and say, "You know, I have - n't seen you a - round
Csus2
3fr
G
be - fore." 'Cause when you're fif - teen
Em7
D
and some - bod - y tells you they love you, you're gon - na be - lieve
C
G
D/F#
them.
And when you're fif - teen, feel - in' like there's noth -
And when you're fif - teen, and your first kiss makes

Em7
Csus2
3fr
Em7
- in' to fig - ure out, well, count to ten, take it in.
your head spin 'round, but, in your life you'll do things
D
G
D/F♯
To Coda
This is life be - fore you know who you're gon - na be.
great - er than dat - in' the boy on the foot - ball team,
C
D
Gsus2
Fif - teen.
Csus2
3fr
Em7
Csus2
3fr

G
C
You sit in class next to a red - head named Ab - i - gail and soon
Em7
C
e - nough you're best friends,
G
C
laugh - in' at the oth - er girls who think they're so cool. We'll be out -
Em7
Csus2
3fr
ta here as soon as we can. And

G
C
then you're on ___ your ver - y first date, ___ and he's got ___ a car, ___
Em7
Csus2
3fr
G
___ and you're feel- in' like fly - in'. ___ And your ma-ma's wait - in' up, ___ and you're
Csus2
3fr
Em7
think - in' he's ___ the one, ___ and you're danc - in' 'round your room ___ when the night ___
C
D/C
C
D.S. al Coda
___ ends, when the night ___ ends. 'Cause when you're

CODA
C
Csus2
3fr
D
G
but I did - n't know it at fif - teen.
C
Em7
C(add9)
D
C
Em7
D
When all you want - ed was to be want - ed, wish you could go back and
G
D/F♯
C
D
Dsus
tell your - self what you know now.

Gsus2
Csus2
3fr
Back then I swore I was gon - na mar - ry him some - day, but I
Em7
Csus2
3fr
re - al - ized some big - ger dreams of mine. And
G
Csus2
3fr
Ab - i - gail gave ev - 'ry - thing she had to a boy
Em7
Csus2
3fr
C
who changed his mind. And we both cried. 'Cause when you're

G
Em7
fif - teen and some - bod - y tells you they love
D
C
you, you're gon - na be - lieve them. And when you're
N.C.
G
D/F#
Em7
fif - teen, don't for - get to look be - fore you fall.
Csus2
3fr
Em7
I've found time can heal most

D
G
D/F♯
an - y - thing, and you just might find who you're sup - posed to be.
C
Em7
D/F♯
C
Csus2
3fr
I did - n't know who I was s'posed to be
D
G
Csus2
3fr
at fif - teen.
Em7
C
La la la la la la la la la la,

G
C
la la la la la la la la la la.
Em7
C
La la la la la la your ver - y first
G
C
day.
Take a deep breath, girl.
Em7
C
Csus2
3fr
Take a deep breath as you walk through the doors.

GETTIN' YOU HOME
(The Black Dress Song)

Words and Music by CHRIS YOUNG,
KENT BLAZY and CORY BATTEN

C
G
C
you love gettin' dressed up and you know I love showin' you off,
by that look in your eyes and your hand drawin' hearts on mine,
G
Am7
G/B
but watchin' your baby blue eyes dancin' in the candlelight
that our night out of the house ain't gonna last too
C
Am
glow, all I can think about
long when all you can think about
D
G
C
G
is gettin' you home.
is gettin' me home.
Walkin' through the

Am
G
front door,
see - in' your black dress hit the floor,
Am
G/B
hon - ey, there sure ain't noth - in' like you lov - in' me
C
Am
To Coda
all night long.
And all I can think a - bout
D
1
G
N.C.
2
G
C
is get - tin' you home.

G
D.S. al Coda
Walk - in' through the
CODA
D
all I can think
Am7
a - bout,
D
all I can think a - bout
Am
D
is get - tin' you home.
G
C
G
Am
D
G
C
G

HERE COMES GOODBYE

Words and Music by CHRIS SLIGH
and CLINT LAGERBERG

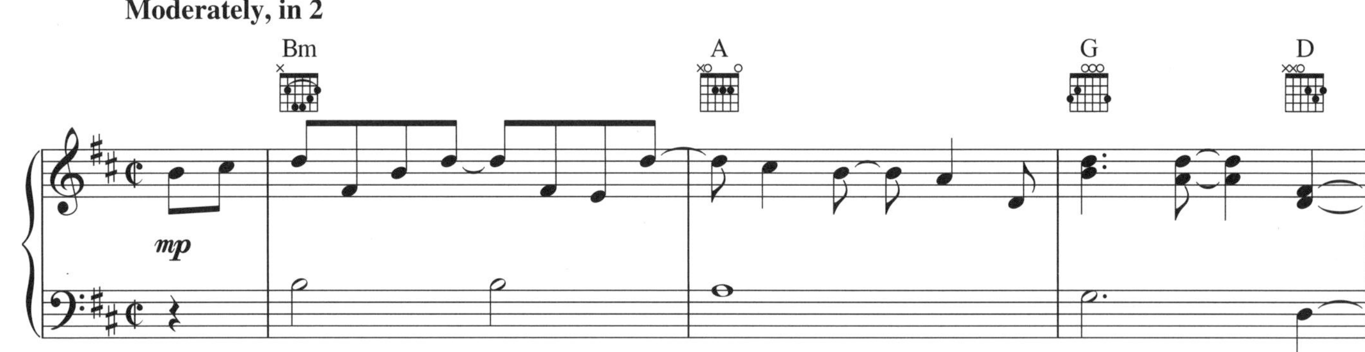

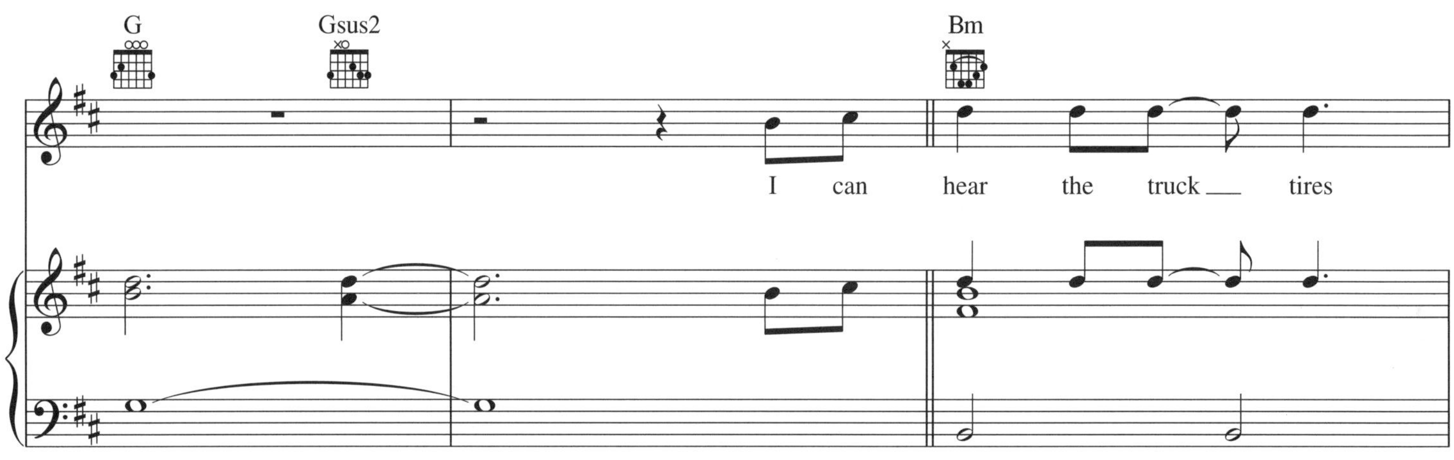

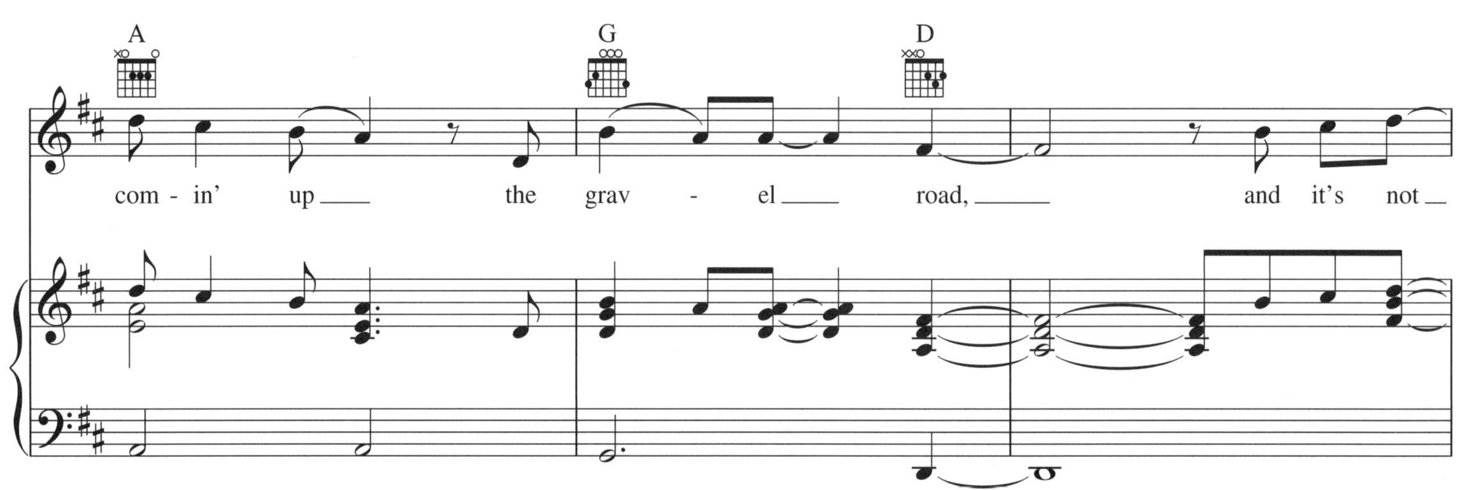

Bm
A
Gsus2
like her to drive that slow; nothin's on the ra-
Bm
A
di - o. Foot-steps on the front porch, I
G
D/F#
Em7
hear my door - bell. She u - sually comes right in.
Asus
Now I can tell, here comes good - bye.

Em7
G
Here comes the last time.
D
Here comes the start of ev - 'ry sleep - less night, the first
C
Em7
of ev - 'ry tear I'm gon - na cry.
mf
G
Here comes the pain.
Here comes me

Bm
A/C♯
D
wish - in' things had nev - er changed and she was right here in
Em7
D/F♯
G
Dmaj7/F♯
my arms to - night.
dim.
Em7
A
Bm
But here comes good - bye.
mp
A
G
D
I can
cresc.

Bm
A
G
D
hear her say, "I love you" like it was yes - ter - day.
mf
And I can see it writ - ten on her face that
she had nev - er felt this way. One day I thought I'd see
D/F♯
her with her dad - dy by her side, and vi - o - lins

Em7
Asus
___ would play "Here ___ Comes the Bride." ___ But
cresc.
Em7
here comes good - bye. ___ Here comes ___ the last ___
f
G
D
___ time. Here comes ___ the start ___ of ev - 'ry sleep -
C
- less night, ___ the first ___ of ev - 'ry tear ___ I'm ___ gon - na cry. ___

Em7
G
Here comes the pain.
Bm
A/C♯
Here comes me wish - in' things had nev - er changed and
D
Em7
D/F♯
G
she was right here in my arms to - night.
D/F♯
Em7
A
But here comes good - bye.

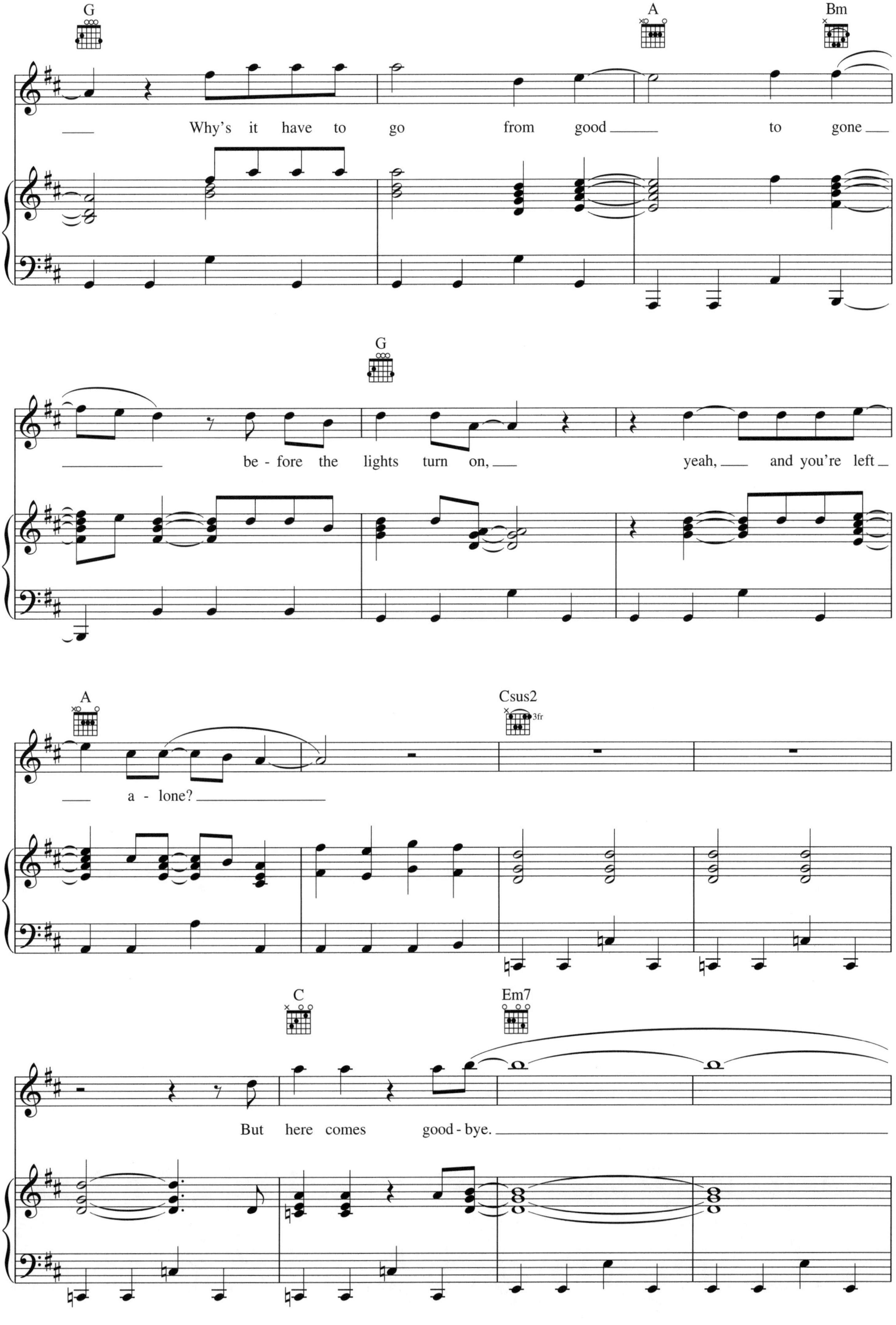
G
A
Bm
Why's it have to go from good to gone
G
before the lights turn on, yeah, and you're left
A
Csus2
alone?
C
Em7
But here comes goodbye.

G
D
A
G
D/F♯
Em7
G
Bm
A
G
Gsus2
G
Here comes good - bye.
dim.
mp

Here comes the last time.
Here comes the start
D
C
of ev - 'ry sleep - less night, the first of ev - 'ry tear
cresc. poco a poco
G
D/F#
Em7
I'm gon - na cry.
Here comes the pain.
f
G
Bm
Here comes me wish - in' things had

A/C♯
D
Em7
D/F♯
nev - er changed and she was right here in my arms
G
D/F♯
Em7
A
to - night.
But here comes
dim.
Bm
A
G
good - bye.
mp
D
Bm
A
Gsus2
molto rit.

I WANNA MAKE YOU CLOSE YOUR EYES

Words and Music by DIERKS BENTLEY
and BRETT BEAVERS

*Recorded a half step lower.

G
D
A
G
I just wan-na lay here and feel you breathe,
lis-ten to the
And if you need a lit-tle bit of help from me,
babe, there's not a
D
A
Em7
G
rhy-thm of your heart beat
and see where it leads.
but-ton that I can't reach.
Let's see where it leads.
D
A
We're wide a-wake, but girl, I wan-na make you close
Em7
G
D
your eyes
and say my name like on-

A
Em7
G
-ly you can say it and hold me tight. (D.S.) Vocal ad lib.
Bm7
A
G
All I need is on-ly you and me a-lone to-night.
To Coda
1
D
F♯m7
I wan-na make you close your eyes, oh.
G
G6
Gmaj7
G
2
C
close your eyes.

G/B
D
I wan-na take you some-where
C
G/B
Em7
D/F♯
Em7
out there till the world fades out of sight.
A
D.S. al Coda
CODA
D
F♯m7
close your eyes, oh.

G
G6
Gmaj7
G
D
I wan - na make you close your eyes,
F♯m7
G
G6
Gmaj7
G
oh.
Girl,
I wan - na make you
D
F♯m7
close your eyes.
G
G6
Gmaj7
G
D

I'M ALIVE

Words and Music by KENNY CHESNEY,
DEAN DILLON and MARK TAMBURINO

E♭
E♭+/G
A♭
3fr
4fr
Ev - 'ry - bod - y's got their share of bat - tle scars.
A♭m
E♭
E♭+/G
As for me, I'd like to thank
A♭
A♭m
E♭
my luck - y stars that I'm a - live
E♭+/G
A♭
A♭m
and well.

E♭
E♭+/G
A♭
It'd be eas - y to add up all the pain
Stars are danc - in' on the wa - ter here to - night.
A♭m
E♭
E♭+/G
and all the dreams you sat and watched
It's good for the soul when there's not
A♭
A♭m
E♭
go up in flames. Dwell on the wreck -
a soul in sight. This boat has caught
E♭+/G
A♭
A♭m
- age as it smol - ders in the rain. But not
its wind and brought me back to life. Now I'm a -

E♭
E♭+/G
A♭
3fr
4fr
me,
live
I'm a - live.
and well.
A♭m
Cm
E♭+/B
And to - day you know that's
E♭/B♭
F7
Cm
6fr
good e - nough for me.
Breath - in' in
E♭+/B
E♭/B♭
F7
and out's a bless - ing, can't you see?

Cm
E♭+/B
E♭/B♭
3fr
6fr
To - day's the first day of the rest of my
F
E♭
E♭+/G
3fr
life and I'm a - live and
A♭
A♭m
E♭
4fr
well.
Yeah, I'm a - live
E♭+/G
A♭
A♭m
and well.
To Coda

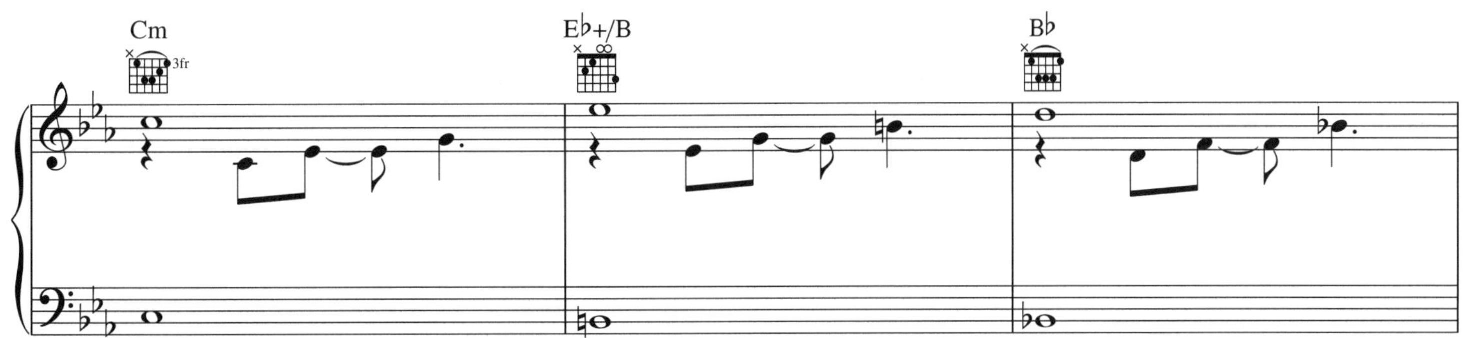
Cm
3fr
E♭+/B
B♭

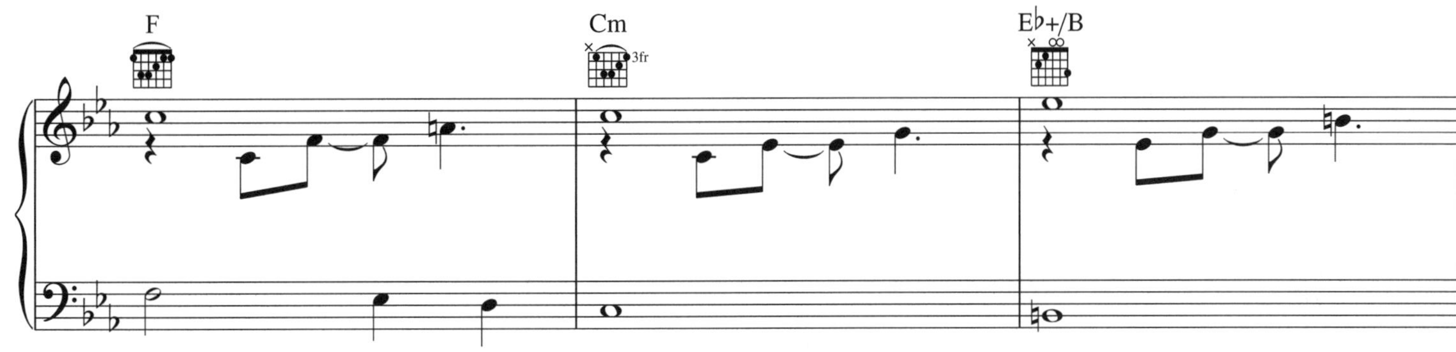
F
Cm
3fr
E♭+/B

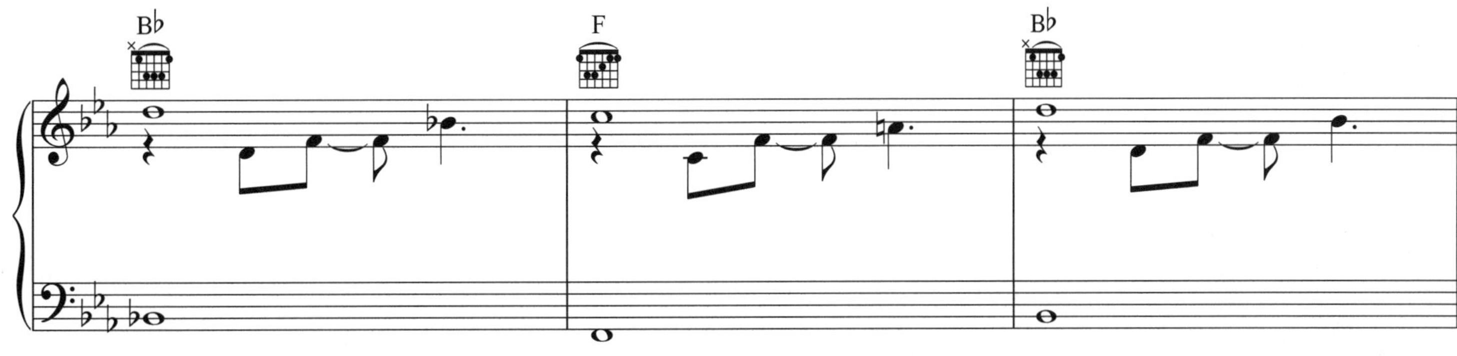
B♭
F
B♭

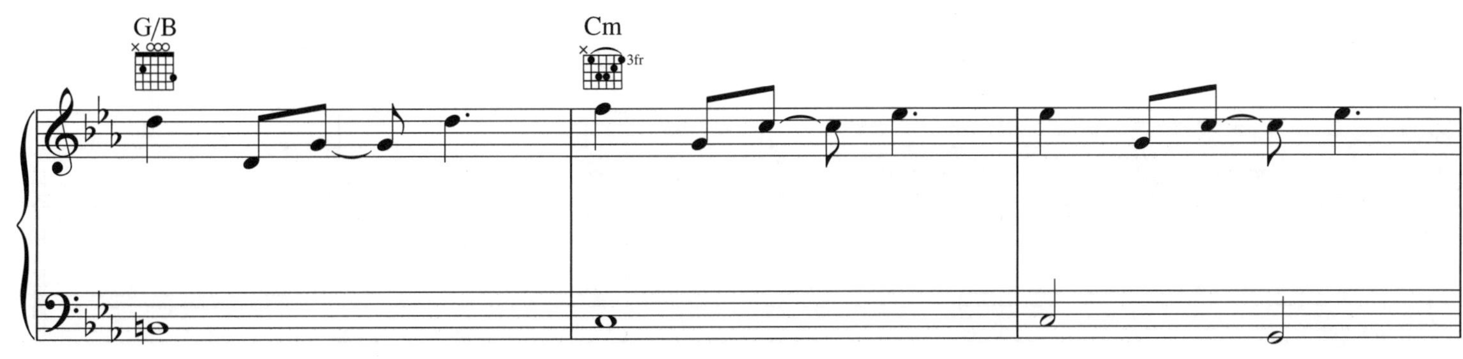
G/B
Cm
3fr

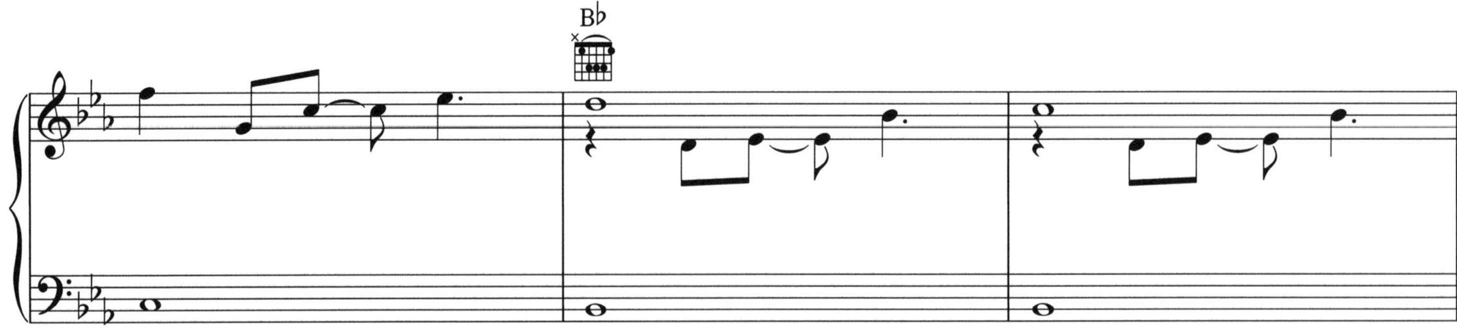
B♭

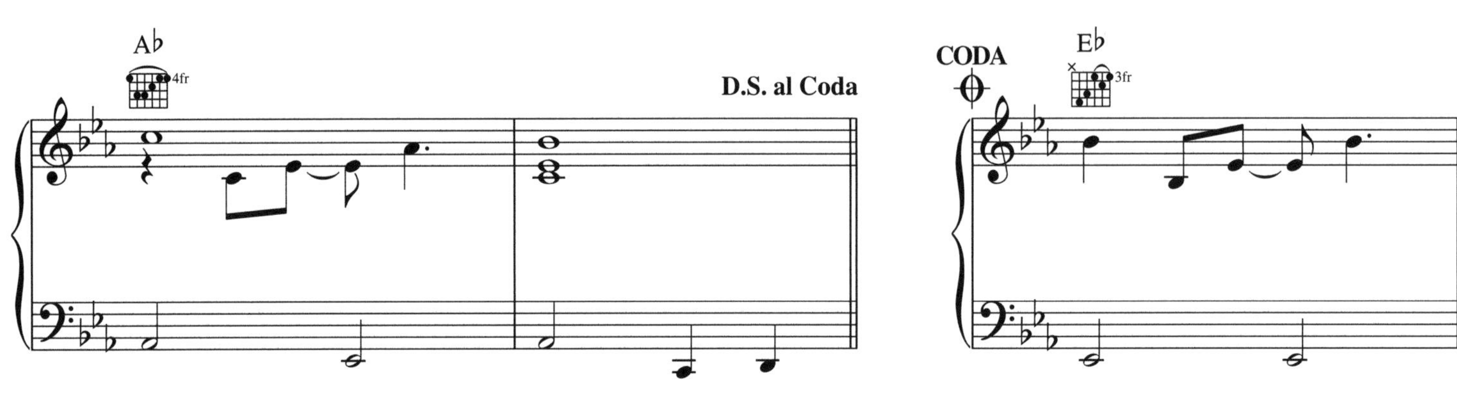
A♭
4fr
D.S. al Coda
CODA
E♭
3fr

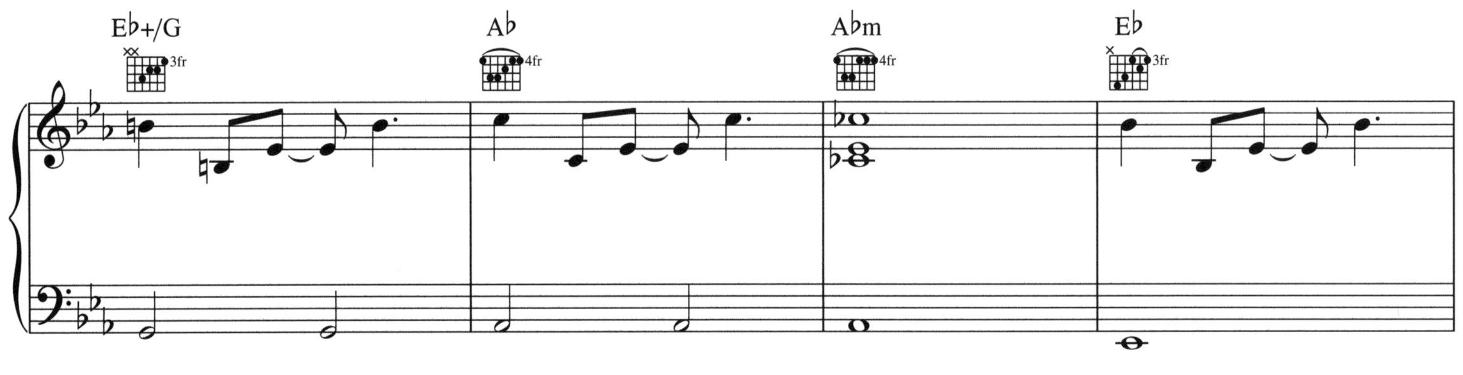
E♭+/G
3fr
A♭
4fr
A♭m
4fr
E♭
3fr

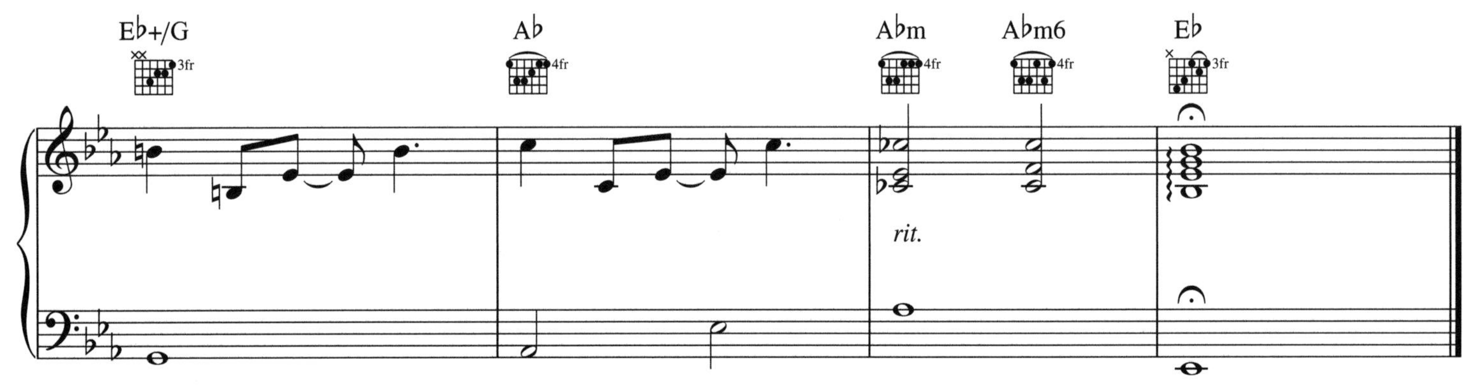
E♭+/G
3fr
A♭
4fr
A♭m
4fr
A♭m6
4fr
E♭
3fr
rit.

TOES

Words and Music by SHAWN MULLINS,
ZAC BROWN, WYATT DURRETTE
and JOHN HOPKINS

*Recorded a half step lower.

G
F
G
beer in my hand. Life is good to - day,
life is good to - day.
C
Well, the plane touched down just a - bout
flew by like a drunk
F
C
three o' - clock and the cit - y's still on my mind.
Fri - day night as the sum - mer drew to an end.
G
C
F
Bi - ki - nis and palm trees danced in my head, I was still
They can't be - lieve that I just could - n't leave, and I bid

C
G
C
in the bag - gage line. Con - crete and cars are their own
a - dieu to my friends. 'Cause my bar - ten - der, she's
F
C
G
pri - son bars like this life I'm liv - in' in. But the
from the is - lands, her bod - y's been kissed by the sun. And
C
F
C
G
plane brought me far - ther, I'm sur - round - ed by wa - ter and I'm not goin' back a - gain.
co - co - nut re - plac - es the smell of the bar, and I don't know if it's her or the rum.
C
F
I got my toes in the wa - ter, ass in the sand, not a wor -

C
Am
G
F
-ry in the world, a cold beer in my hand. Life is good to-day,
G
C
N.C.
3
life is good to-day.
A-di-os and va-ya con
3
F
C
Di-os,
yeah, I'm leav-in' G-A.
a long way from G-A.
go-in' home now to stay.
G
And if it weren't for te-qui-la and
Yes, and all the mu-cha-chas, they
The se-ño-ri-tas don't care-o when

G7
pret - ty se - ño - ri - tas, I'd have no rea - son to
call me big pa - pa when I throw pe - sos their
there's no di - ne - ro. I got no mon - ey to
C
N.C.
F
stay.
way.
stay.
A - di - os and va - ya con Di - os,
C
To Coda
yeah, I'm leav - in' G - A. Gon - na
a long way from G - A. Some - one
go - in' home now to stay.
G
G7
lay in the hot sun and roll a big fat one and,
do me a fa - vor and pour me some Jae - ger and

N.C.
C
F
and grab my gui - tar and play.
I'll grab my gui - tar and play.
C
G
C
F
C
G
1
C
The four days
2
C
F/C
C
N.C.
D.S. al Coda
A - di - os and va - ya con
3
3
3
3
3

CODA
G
(Spoken:) Just gonna drive up by the lake and put my
C
F/C
ass in a lawn chair, toes in the clay, not a wor -
C
Am
G
F
- ry in the world, a P - B - R on the way. Life is good to - day,
G
C
F
G
C
life is good to - day.

NEED YOU NOW

Words and Music by HILLARY SCOTT,
CHARLES KELLEY, DAVE HAYWOOD
and JOSH KEAR

A
C♯m
4fr
-der if I ev - er crossed your mind.
A
For me it hap - pens all the time. It's a
E
quar - ter af - ter one,
(1.,D.S.) I'm all a - lone
(2.) I'm a lit - tle drunk
and I need
G♯m
4fr
you now.
Said

E
I would - n't call, (1.,2.) but I lost all con - trol and I need
(D.S.) but I'm a lit - tle drunk
G♯m
4fr
you now. And I don't
A
know how I can do with - out. I
To Coda
1
just need you now.

C♯m
4fr
An -
2
C♯m
4fr
B
E
A
B
C♯m
4fr
3
B
E
A
B
A
Guess I'd rath - er hurt than feel

C♯m
4fr
B
D.S. al Coda
noth - in' at all.
It's a
CODA
E
G♯m
4fr
E
I just need you now.
G♯m
4fr

E
G♯m
4fr
Oh, __ ba -
- by, I need __ you now. __
E
G♯m
4fr
E
Emaj7

RED LIGHT

Words and Music by DENNIS MATKOSKY,
JONATHAN SINGLETON and MELISSA PIERCE

D
like.
F♯m
A
It ain't the mid-dle of the night,
F♯m
A
and it ain't e - ven rain - in' out - side.
F♯m
A
It ain't ex - act - ly what I had in mind

D
A/C♯
Bm7
for good - bye.
D
A
E
F♯m
At a red light in the sun - shine, on a Sun - day, noth - in' to say;
But at a red light in the sun - shine, it was Sun - day. Noth - in' to say;
D
A
E
don't e - ven try.
don't e - ven try.
D
A
E
F♯m
Some are com - in' home, some are leav - in' town while my world's crash - in' down

To Coda
D
A
E
on a Sun - day in the sun - shine,
at a red light.
D
A
E/A
A
D
A
F♯m
A
I thought she was gon - na say
some - thin' 'bout that cou -

F♯m
A
- ple kiss - in', cross - in' the street, or some - thin' a - bout this beau - ti - ful day.
F♯m
A
But she just looked me in the eye, said it's o - ver, did - n't
F♯m
A
try to lie or pick a fight. I might-'ve seen it
D
A/C♯
Bm7
D.S. al Coda
com - in' that way.

CODA
E
D
at a red light.
There's a ma-ma calm-in' down a lit-tle ba-by in the back seat in front of me. There's an
old man dressed in his Sun-day best just wait-in' on green.
But I
Bm7
can't see get-tin' past

D
A
E
F♯m
this red light in the sun - shine, on a Sun - day. Noth - in' to say;
At a red light in the sun - shine, on a Sun - day, noth - in' to say;
D
A
E
don't e - ven try.
don't e - ven try.
D
A
E
F♯m
Some are com - in' home, some are leav - in' town while my world's crash - in' down
D
A
1
E
on a Sun - day
in the sun - shine.
in the sun - shine,

2
E
D
at a red light,
A
E/A
A
D
at a red light,
A
E/A
A
D
at a red light,
A
E/A
A
D
A
at a red light.

SMALL TOWN USA

Words and Music by JUSTIN MOORE,
JEREMY STOVER and BRIAN MAHER

* *Recorded a half step higher.*

F
C/E
B♭
B♭sus2
B♭
But these are my roots and this is what I love.
We nev - er get a - head but we have e - nough.
'Cause ev - 'ry - bod - y knows me and I know them and I be -
I watch peo - ple leave and then come right back.
lieve that's the way we're sup - posed to live. I would-n't trade one
I nev - er want - ed an - y part of that. And I'm proud to say I
C
sin - gle day here in
love this place, good ol'
N.C.
Small Town U - S - A.

B♭/F
F
Give me a Sat - ur - day night, my ba - by
C/E
B♭
by my side, a lit - tle Hank Jun - ior
Da - vid Al - lan Coe
Sweet Home Al - a - bam - a
and a six - pack of light, an
F
C/E
B♭
old dirt road and I'll be just fine.
C
F
C/E
Give me a Sun - day morn - in' that's full of grace,
3

To Coda
Dm7
B♭
F/A
B♭
a sim - ple life and I'll be o - kay, here in Small Town
1
C
F
C/E
U - S - A.
B♭
B♭sus2
B♭
2
C
U - S -
F
C/E
B♭
A, oh, yeah.

C
F
C/E
B♭
C
B♭
I would-n't trade one
sin - gle day,
C/B♭
B♭
rath - er say I
love this place.
C
D.S. al Coda
Give me a
CODA
B♭
be o - kay.
3

F/A
B♭
C
Yeah, I'll be o - kay here in Small Town U - S - A.
F
C
B♭
Oh, yeah, Small
C
F
C
Town U - S - A.
B♭
C
F

SOUTHERN VOICE

Words and Music by TOM DOUGLAS
and BOB DiPIERO

D
A
ly Par - ton graced __ it,
tor King __ paved __ it,
Ros - a Parks rode __ it,
Bear Bry - ant won __ it,
E
A
Scar - lett O chased __ it. __
Bil - ly Gra - ham saved it. __
Smooth as the
D
A
E
hick - 'ry wind __ that blows from Mem-phis down to Ap - a - lach - i - co - la,
A
D
A
it's "Hi, y'all. Did __ ya eat __ well?
Come on in. __ I'm
(D.S.) Come on in, __ child.

E
D
E
sure glad to know ya."
Sure glad to know ya."
Don't let this old gold cross and this
A
D
A
All - man Broth - ers t - shirt throw ya.
Crim - son Tide t - shirt throw ya.
Char - lie Dan - iels t - shirt throw ya.
It's ci - ca - das mak - in' noise
It's ci - ca - das mak - in' noise
We're just boys mak - in' noise
E
To Coda
1
D
with a South - ern voice.
A
D
A

D
2 D
Hank
A
D
A
E
A
D
A
E
A
Je - sus is my friend,

D
A
D
A - mer - i - ca is my home.
E
Sweet iced tea and Jer - ry Lee,
Day - to - na Beach, that's what
gets to me. I can feel it in my bones.
D.S. al Coda
CODA
D
A
Yeah, yeah, yeah, yeah,

D
A
D
Southern voice.
I got a Southern voice,
A
D
A
Southern voice.
D
A
D
A
D
A

'TIL SUMMER COMES AROUND

Words and Music by MONTY POWELL
and KEITH URBAN

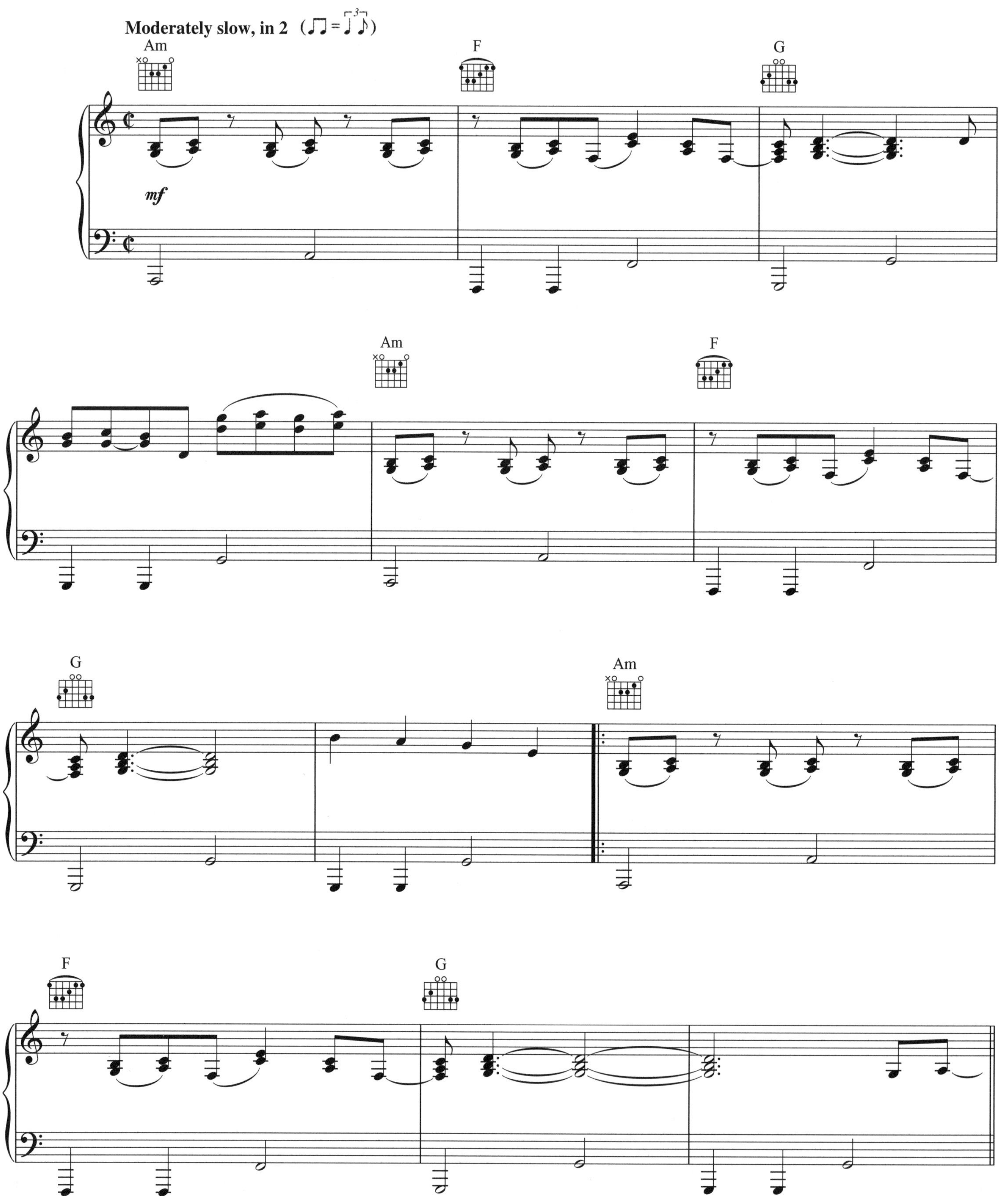

Am
F
G
An - oth - er long sum - mer's come and gone.
I got a job work - ing at the old park pier,
Am
F
I don't know why it al - ways ends
and ev - 'ry sum - mer now for five
G
Am
this way.
long years
The board - walk's
I grease the gears, fix the lights,
F
G
qui - et and the car - ni - val rides
tight - en bolts, straight - en the tracks,
3
3

Fsus2
are as emp - ty as my bro - ken heart to - night.
and I count the days 'til you just might come back.
G
Fmaj7
But I
And then I
close my eyes and one
C
G
more time we're spin - ning a - round and you're hold - ing on
Fmaj7
C
tight - ly. The words came out; I kissed your mouth. No Fourth

G
of Ju - ly has ev - er burned so bright - ly. You
Fmaj7
C
G
had to go; I un - der - stand.
But you prom - ised you'd be back a - gain,
But you swore that you'd be back a - gain,
Fsus2
and so I wan - der 'round this town
and so I'm fro - zen in this town
G
1.
Am
'til sum - mer comes a - round.
'til

F
G
2.
Am
F
sum - mer comes a - round.
G
Am
Fsus2
G
Am
F
G

Am
Fsus2
G
Fmaj7
Oh, and I close my eyes and you
C
G
and I are stuck on the Fer - ris wheel, rock - in' with the mo - tion. And
Fmaj7
C
hand in hand, we cried and laughed, know - ing that love

G
C/E
G
Fmaj7
belonged to us, girl, if only for a moment. And "Baby, I'll be back
C
G
again," you whispered in my ear. But now the winter wind is the
Fsus2
G
only sound,
Fsus2
and ev'rything is closing down

G
Am
'til sum - mer comes a - round,
F
G
'til sum - mer comes a - round.
Am
F
G
3
Am
F
G
Repeat and Fade

WHY

Words and Music by ROBERT MATHES
and ALLEN SHAMBLIN

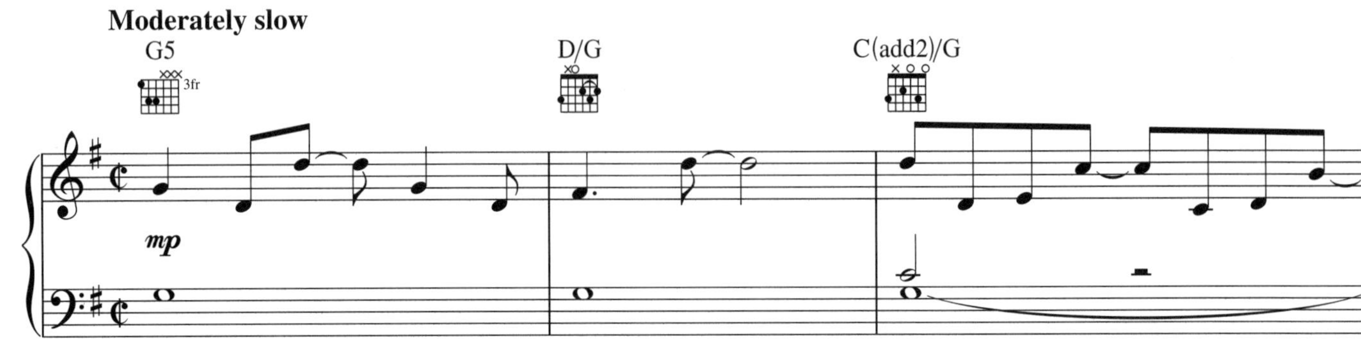

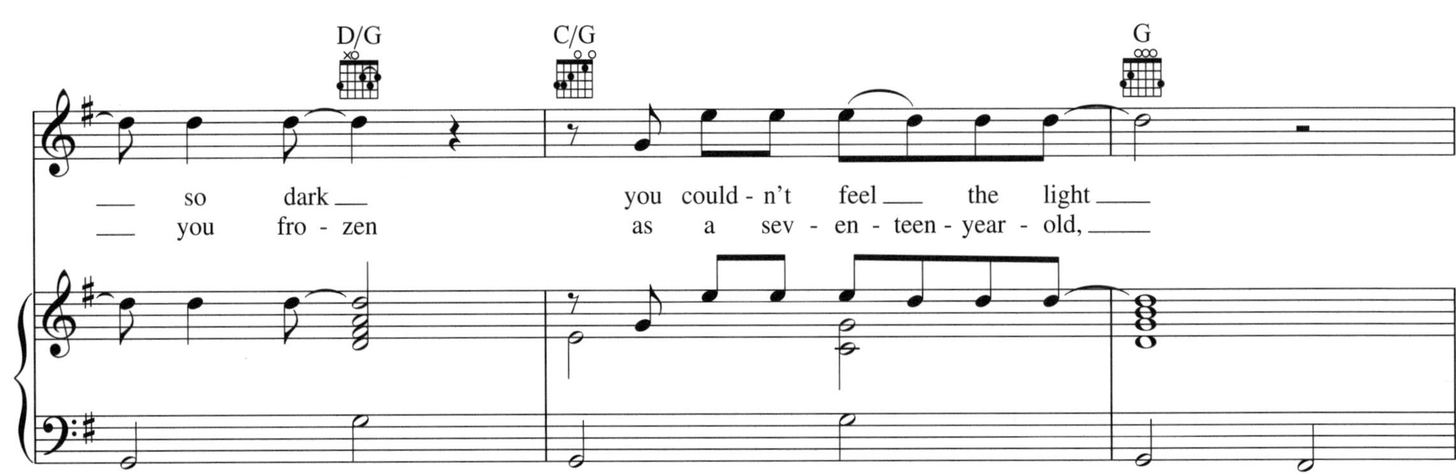

Em7
D
C
reach - in' for you through that storm - y cloud.
round - ing third to score the win - ning run.
G
Gmaj7
Now here we are gath - ered in our
You al - ways played with pas - sion no
C/G
G
G/D
lit - tle home town.
This can't be the way you meant
mat - ter what the game.
When you took the stage, you'd shine
D
C
G
to draw a crowd.
just like the sun.
Oh,

Bm7
C
why? That's what I keep ask -
G
- ing. Was there an - y - thing I could have
D
Bm7
said or done? Oh, I
C
had no clue you were mask - ing a

G
D
Dsus
trou - bled soul.
God on - ly knows
D
Em
G/B
what went wrong
and why
C
G/B
Am7
you would leave the stage in the
1
D7sus
G5
3fr
D/G
mid - dle of a song.

C(add2)/G
G5
3fr
D/G
C(add2)/G
Now
2
D
Em
D
mid - dle
of a song.
C
Em
Bm/D

C
G/B
A7sus
A
A7sus
A
G/B
C
Csus2
3fr
G
Now the oak trees are sway - in' in the
C/G
G
Em
ear - ly au - tumn breeze, a gold - en sun is shin -

D
C(add2)
-in' on my face. Through
G
C/G
tan-gled thoughts I hear a mock-ing-bird sing.
G
G/D
D
This old world real-ly ain't that bad a place.
C
G/B
G
Bm7
Oh, why?

C
There's no com - pre - hend - ing and
G
D
who am I to try to judge or ex - plain?
Bm7
Oh, but I do have one burn -
C
G/D
- ing ques - tion: Who told you life

D
wasn't worth the fight?
They were wrong.
Em
Bm/D
C
They lied.
3
Em
Bm/D
Now you're gone and we
C
G/B
Am7
cry 'cause it's not like you

D7sus
G5
3fr
to walk a - way in the mid - dle of a song
Gmaj7
C(add2)/G
G5
3fr
your beau - ti - ful song.
D/G
C(add2)/G
G
Your ab - so - lute - ly
Gmaj7
C(add2)/G
G
beau - ti - ful song.
rit.

YOU BELONG WITH ME

Words and Music by TAYLOR SWIFT
and LIZ ROSE

* Recorded a half step lower.

G
D
I'm in the room, it's a typ - i - cal Tues-day night. I'm lis - t'nin' to the kind of
Am7
mu - sic she does - n't like. And she'll nev - er know your sto - ry like
C
Am7
I do.
But she wears short skirts,
She wears high heels,
C
G
D
I wear T - shirts.
I wear sneak - ers.
She's cheer cap - tain and I'm on the bleach - ers,

Am7
C
D
dream-in' 'bout the day when you wake up and find __ that what you're look-in' for __ has been here __
G
__ the whole time. If you could see that I'm __ the one __ who un-der-stands you.
D
Am7
Been here all __ a-long. __ So why can't you see __
To Coda
C
__ you be-long __ with me? __ You be-long __ with me. __

G
Walk - in' the streets with you
in your worn - out jeans,
D
I can't help think - in' this is how it ought to be.
Am7
Laugh - in' on a park bench, think - in' to my - self,
C
"Hey, is - n't this eas - y?"
And you've
G
got a smile that could light up this whole town.

D
Am7
I have-n't seen it in a while since she brought you down. You say you're fine. I know you
C
D.S. al Coda
bet - ter than that. Hey, what you do - in' with a girl like that?
CODA
C
G
me? Stand - in' by and wait-
D
Am7
- in' at your back door. All this time how could you not know, ba - by,

C
you be - long with
me?
You be - long with me.
G
D
Am7
C
Am7
Oh, I re - mem - ber you
driv - in' to my house in the

C
G
mid - dle of the night. I'm the one who makes you laugh when you
D
Am7
know you're 'bout to cry. I know your fav - 'rite songs and you
C
G
tell me 'bout your dreams. Think I know where you be - long. Think I
D
G
know it's with me. Can't you see that I'm the one

D/F#
who un-der-stands you? Been here all a-long. So why can't you
Am7
C
see you be-long with me?
G
Stand-in' by here, wait-in' at your back door.
D
Am7
All this time how could you not know, ba-by,

C
you be - long with
me?
You be - long with me.
G
D
You be - long with me.
Have you
Am7
ev - er thought just may - be
you be - long with
C
G
me?
You be - long with me.